FROM BEING A CHURCH GOER,

TO BECOMING THE ORDAINED DEACON, I NOW AM.

Yes, A Servant For Life, I Now Am.

Certificate of Baptism

This Certifies That

Eugene Frederick Martin

Child of Thomas

and his wife Eugenia

Born at Grady Hospital Atlanta Ga.

Date of birth Aug. 22nd 1947

Was baptized in Mt Zion

Methodist Church

On the 27th day of April

In the year of our Lord 1952

in the Name of the Father and of the Son

and of the Holy Ghost

Witnesses Mary C. Still

Beatrice Pierce

Edgar V. Wimberly

Pastor

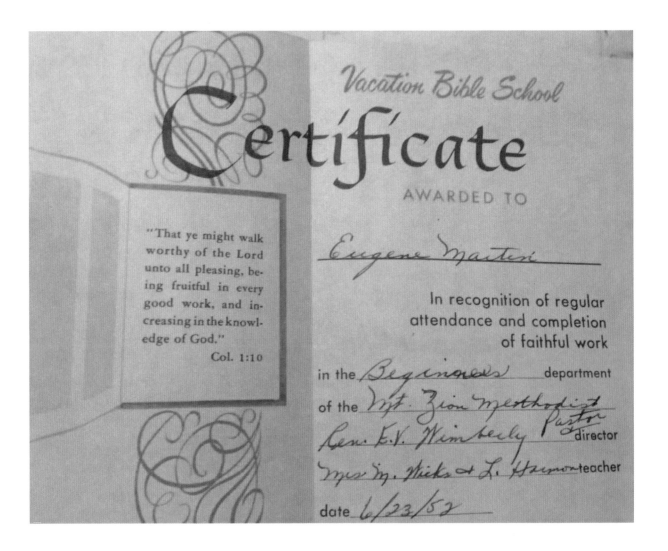

Vacation Bible School **Certificate** AWARDED TO

"That ye might walk worthy of the Lord unto all pleasing, being fruitful in every good work, and increasing in the knowledge of God."
Col. 1:10

Eugene Martin

In recognition of regular attendance and completion of faithful work

in the *Beginners* department

of the *Mt. Zion Methodist*

Rev. E.V. Wimberly Pastor/director

Mrs. M. Hicks & L. Harmon teacher

date *6/23/52*

It was two years before my youngest brother Samuel's birth, that on April 27, 1952, our dad, Thomas Allen Martin arranged for us kids, Beatrice, Elsie, Thomas Junior, and myself to be baptized at the church he wanted us as a family to attend. I remember the minister, Pastor Edgar Wimberly, holding Thomas Junior who was then less then one year old, head over a Baptismal Bowl as he sprinkled water over his head and spoke words. This he did with each of us kids one by one.

Vacation Church School

This Certificate of Recognition

is awarded to Eugene Martin

for satisfactory work and regular attendance

in the Beginners Department of the Vacation Church School

of Mt. Zion Methodist Church

at Lawnside N.J. Winifred Still
TEACHER

June 8 to June 26 1953 C. Still
DATE OF SCHOOL DIRECTOR

Mount Zion United Methodist Church in Lawnside, New Jersey became my first

introduction to how to try and live a Godly life. During times afterwards I

remember dad taking me to Boy Scout meetings he helped with at the church,

allowing me to meet other males who attended, some my age who also were

there with dads. I enjoyed how he would take me with the Boy Scouts on hikes

throughout the town and towns around.

   During Sunday school at the church, I still remember each child in my class,

learning different scriptures and at the end of the class, all children in

attendance would get a small post card with a biblical picture associated with

the lesson that was taught to us to take home. To this very day, I still own a couple of mine, because my mom was one who made sure that each of us kids would have a baby book of our childhood and the things we each did as children, to look back over years later. I also remember that during certain occasions, I had to recite verses in front of a gathering of people who also attended for what the occasion was. Christmas, Easter, etc. Me being a shy child, did not like to have to stand and do this, but did so in obedience to my parents.

Then one dad my dad passed from an illness he had for a while, that changed our family life, us kids now not having a two parent household. I remember the day of the funeral at the church, and for the first time in my life seeing a person laid out in a casket. I stood looking at dad with tears running down my face. Seeing my dad lifeless, with his eyes closed like he was sleeping, has been a moment I will never forget. During the service people would walk pass my mom and us kids, as they also got to view him laying there. Reverend Wimberly spoke words at the service and afterwards everyone got into vehicles to travel the many miles to a cemetery. I remember looking back at the long line of vehicles following us, and to me there were so many with lights on who wanted to come along. As we approached the military plot prepared for him with soldiers there, probably the same ones who folded his flag that was draped over the casket at the church, and after folding it, gave the flag to my mom. At the gravesite, words were said and I along with the others, I watched his casket being lowered into the deepest hole I had ever seen. Afterwards, it was back home for us,

going to 221 White Horse Pike.

SUMMER VACATION BIBLE SCHOOLS

During my summer vacation, us older household children would attend Mount

Zion for our vacation bible school sessions. My mom was one of the teachers of

older kids then me there, and I was in a different class, with other youth around

my age. I attended those sessions for years, before us being invited to also

attend our neighborhood family's church, a very close friendly family who

assisted my parents all during our moving into 221. The Robert and Mary

Corsey family, attended an Episcopal Church (Chapel of Annunciation also in Lawnside, New Jersey) and by my attending vacation bible study there, the pastor of that church made an arrangement for me to at times be an alter boy during some services that were held there. I learned how to march towards the alter in formation, light candles, and properly put them out at the end of service. I learned to position my bent knees on the small bench, and recite words from a book in the pew for all to lift up and recite from, as all did at the proper time. In attending this church I got to meet other children of my age, now meeting kids from two churches and being called upon from both churches, often when needed.

Because both of these churches were not in the town we lived in, but the town next to us, and mom now wanting us kids to attend a church closer to our home, we started attending a Baptist church just blocks away, Mount Olive Baptist Church here in Magnolia, under the teachings of Reverend Hampton. Just like the Sunday school classes I had attended in the other churches, I was put in a class with others close to my age and each Sunday learning more of scriptures and how to live as God wanted us to. It was here I was asked to participate in the youth choir with kids my age and older, and some even younger. I had been singing at events for some churches as a soloist for some time, so getting an opportunity to sing with many others was a welcome, me still being shy and nervous often. Over the course of time, us kids attending Sunday school service, were called upon many times to participate in just about any area the leaders saw we could help in. Bea had for years been taking piano lessons and was really good at reading and playing music. She enjoyed playing and would practice almost daily from a hymn book the church allowed her to keep at our home. Penny also could read music after taking lessons over time and she also would sometimes play for the Sunday school and even once she played for myself and two others friends of mine, us trying to start a little singing group. For a short period of time, Thomas Junior took lessens and when the leader of the Sunday school found out that he was taking lessons, allowed him to have a chance of adding his name to the Martin children's piano playing in church. All I will mention is, me and Sammy laugh to this very day, hearing what

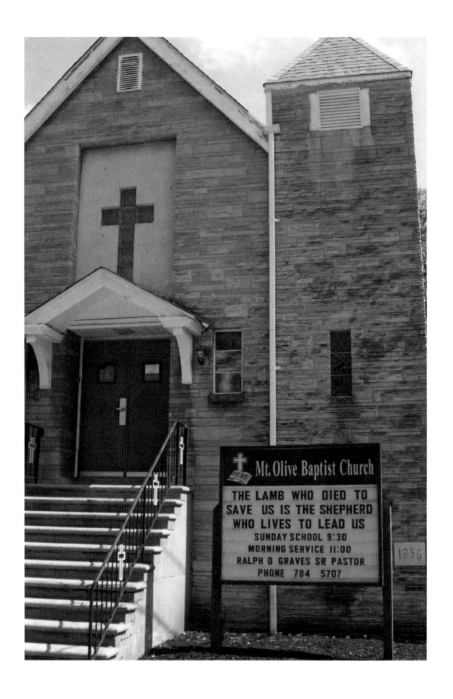

we heard, and seeing the expression on his face looking back at us rolling in our seats laughing with tears in our eyes. He couldn't wait to hurry home and tell mom how Sammy and I acted. The punishment mom put to me was worth the behavior though it badly hurt. That was Tom's first and last time playing for any service in church especially knowing that Sammy and I would be in attendance.

Every Easter and Christmas, each of us were given what were called pieces to memorize and be ready to recite during an evening gathering for members to participate in a play performance or a choice of something else, but everyone had to do something. Each time I was told I had to recite a piece, I was made to recite one that had more than one verse, which is what I wanted. They made me do at least three verses, and every occasion, I struggled in learning them. My sister Bea use to tick me off because she and her girlfriends would in my opinion, challenge each other to who could recite the most verses. I don't think she ever had less than twelve and would make me mad, remembering every line with ease. All her girlfriends could do that. We had to sit and listen to at least six of those girls do that at every occasion. Somewhere in between one of them girls, my name would be called to recite mine, and the sweat would be rolling on my forehead knowing mom, who always made sure she would sit way in the back of the church, daring us to not talk loud enough for her to hear us recite, and better not embarrass her. I fumbled with those pieces every time. I disliked doing that and I won't say I promised, but I made sure any children of mine that God allowed me to have in the future, me becoming an adult parent, I would not put them through doing pieces if they chose not to, and I never did with the two sons I have.

I got strong, sound bible teaching in my childhood, and those teachings helped me all while going to grade school and on to college. I can say that from my late years of grade school and all throughout high school, I hardly ever missed Sunday school and on occasion Morning church as well.

After meeting my girlfriend and future wife Delphine, she told my mom in a conversation while I was away in Chicago, hoping to further my education, Delphine spoke to my mom of her devotion to her Christian way of living, and that she attended church regularly. Her teachings came at a Pentecostal church she was a part of for most of her life. She asked my mom to not mention any of what she was telling my mom to me, but instead to let her do so. When she did tell me and let me know of her Holiness background of teachings, I asked her what was her fear in telling me all what she was telling me now? Her reply was the fear of me not wanting to be associated with her. She let me know of her experience, of how often being found out of her biblical teachings, the word Pentecostal caused people to not want to be associated with her and those she fellowshipped with. Her telling me that bought back a memory of me and one of my older adult family members sitting in front of the television on a Sunday night, the two of us watching a group called the Clara Ward Singer about to sing, and the adult sitting with me voicing that they were, "Holy Rollers". I had never heard those words before and after listening to them sing and me enjoying what I had heard and saw, wondered what was wrong how they clapped and performed. I enjoyed them and if the chance came for me to hear them again, I without hesitation would. So when Delphine told me of her fear of letting me know of her beliefs, I assured her not to worry about her teachings with me.

It was during a time that I was home from college, Delphine invited me to

attend a service that was to held at her church. She told me that every so often,

she would attend a service called "Joy Night ". Different Holiness churches

would get together and have a time of fellowship, hearing preaching and choirs singing in praise to God. I of course accepted and together we went. I had never been to a church as what I was about to experience and had no idea what I was about to see and hear. I remember that the closer we got to the front door walking towards the church, I could hear the uplifting music and voices singing inside. As we entered the first set of doors, the music had stopped and talking from the front was being heard as someone was as I learned, testifying of how good God was to the person speaking. Delphine held my hand to keep me from entering the second set of doors to get to some seats, and let me know to wait till a song was starting, that being the time to enter. She lead me to sit sort of in the middle of the church on a row ahead of others. I could feel eyes upon me as we walked in together and us sitting down. During the months of our relationship, I got to meet a couple of friends of Delphine and she told me that they also attended the church, so when I looked and saw them I kind of felt more relaxed. Now if you read my previous books, you know I had no fear in having to physically defend myself without question, so I was ready for what I believe whatever, I had to defend myself of. Delphine, I am sure was concerned with how this new way of life in praising God, I would handle.   I really enjoyed myself even though I paid attention to all my surroundings with caution.

Her church at that time was preparing to move across the city to its new building where they would fellowship. They did move while I was back in Chicago and upon my returning I would sometimes attend with her. The members had by now knew, Delphine and I were a serious couple, and welcomed me with open arms each time I came to a service. I must admit that I truly felt the love of how I was being approached and accepted..

After Delphine and I got married, we would occasionally fellowship with another family church, and they as well followed Pentecostal beliefs. Because of them being family, we would occasionally take our sons or sometimes I would go alone while Del took the sons to her still home church. At the family church, I was given every opportunity to participate and would do so if I was lead by God. This went on over many months of me bouncing from church to church.

Then God Directed My Path Differently.

One day while I was in the front yard of our home, I saw a neighbor sitting across the street reading on her front steps. Now I have been friends with Janice Watson for many years and though she was my sister Penny's friend as well, Janice was invited to many of the events at 221.   We considered each other as brother and sister. She was always a special individual to me because of her kind personality to everyone. I walked across the street after seeing her on the steps and she invited me to sit down on the step just lower than the one she was sitting on. We began a conversation and somewhere during our talks, Janice asked me, "Genie, have every accepted Jesus as your Personal Savior"? I remember looking at her and telling her that I had never called out to Him as so. We held hands and before us letting go, prayed softly, yet with conviction.

All I can say is my walk back across the highway has never been the same. That experience definitely was a Change in my life.

Over time, I knew I had to get settled in a church home as the adult I was, and stop bouncing from building to building. I made up my mind, as God was leading me, to be obedient and find a church home as fast as I could.

Now since I knew where I was joining and it was not to be at the family church, I felt I should let the family church leader know of what I was about to do. I sat in my relatives living room and told him face to face. He could see that I had made my choice, and his response kind of threw me back. He said, " I took all the time to teach you, me doing all that, and you are not joining my congregation? ". Whatever was said after those words I do not remember. I do know that I learned a long time ago, of the scripture telling us that it is God who increases, after we speak His Word to others. That is an experience I will always remember. Yes, I met some wonderful people in his congregation, mainly the youth who seemed to be excited whenever I was in their church presence, and really excited when I had wife and sons in attendance with me. It was God who was directing me to go and join the church where I was about to go.

I started attending the Mt. Olive Baptist church on the corner near the house, it being the church I attended, while I was in elementary and high school. In a

very short time I joined and was baptized. I knew I was trusting God and doing

the right thing, when I got baptized.

Now because I had been fellowshipping with other churches and I had

listened to members tell of them getting baptized in a creek or what I once

witnessed, in a pool inside a church, and watching the person inch their way

into what I considered cold water, I felt the goosebumps, me disliking cold water. I took the necessary classes leading up to my time to be baptized and the closer it got, the more I had to prepare my mind about the water being too cold. That night of the service, the Deacons had me put on a gown, I stepped up to enter the water in the church pool with my mind made up that no matter how cold the water would be, I was not turning back. I stepped in the water and to my surprise, the water was not cold at all and quite warm. I was one happy person. My prayer was answered about the water not being cold during my "open confession", letting others know that I too had excepted Jesus as my Personal Savior.

Days later while talking to another older member and me telling that God answered my prayer about the water, that person added in, " if you would have asked, someone would had told you that the water is always warm for baptism ceremony in this church. What?

After being a member for many months, one day I was asked to come into the pastor's office, for he wanted to speak to me. I agreed to do so and in conversation he asked if I would accept the calling of being on the trustee board. He explained what was required of the duties and I accepted. I felt honored that the church allowed me to handle money and at times find ways to invest monies in banks in both New Jersey, Pennsylvania, and other states that had high interest rates for short periods of time. I did that often and the church was pleased with the results after they agreed with my decisions after discussion.

Delphine was still a member of the Pentecostal church, but would occasionally come to service with me. When I was asked to be a teacher for one of the vacation bible school classes for a summer, Delphine even gave me suggestions for my teachings. I felt good at the end of the summer teachings and how the youth seemed to have learned and would reach out to me for answers to their questions. It fell good.

Now though I was enjoying my church life there, my hope was that one day Delphine and I would be members of a church we would both join and attend. She was not going to become a member of my church because of it being too laidback in worship and praise to what she was accustomed to. She would attend service at my church and felt out of place with her hand clapping and other forms of praise she didn't hold back on. Over the pool pit at one service, it was told that it didn't take all of that form in praising God, by shouting or hand clapping loudly in praising Him, and she took those words very personal. She was being led to find another place to worship and this was not where she would feel accepted and I definitely agreed with her. My hope was one day she would find a place where she would feel comfortable and at the same time, me as well, that we would be worshipping together in the same congregation.

It was months later while she was traveling with the choir she had joined that was under the care and direction of a known national gospel singing family, she let me know that after visiting a church under the leadership of someone, also a friend of some of her choir members, and he becoming the new pastor of the church, she visited, and in time became a member. The pastor was leading a Baptist congregation but he grew up with a Pentecostal background. After her telling me that she joined, I went to a service with her and after doing so thanked God that He opened a door to my prayer.

Because of me being a trustee and loving the people who I had come to respect and enjoy fellowshipping with, there was no way I would leave them without telling them the reason from my mouth and it not being hearsay, of why I left, and not from anyone else. On a Sunday morning before service was to start, I asked to speak to my pastor and told him of my decision to leave and begin to fellowship with my wife and her decision. He asked me if I knew what I was about to walk into, and I just nodded yes, really not knowing what he was meaning.

All I wanted was just a couple of minutes to speak to the congregation about my decision and say goodbye to them, which the pastor allowed me the time to do. I said what I said to the congregation, and immediately exited out the church by going down the back staircase and out the basement door. I than went and found my wife who had already left for her service and when I entered, saw where she was sitting and sat next to her. After enjoying all that I heard and the pastor opening the door for anyone to become a member, I made my way up. The pastor asked me one question and I gave him my answer. He then had one of the Deacons to take me in a room with him where we introduced

ourselves to each other. He then talked to me and afterwards held out his hand

telling me he was going to say a prayer. I immediately stopped him from

beginning the prayer and told him that it was me who was going to pray, and not

him. Him not disagreeing, I remember talking to my Jesus. After doing so I saw

him smile and we exited the room. Weeks later I was given the right hand of

fellowship from the leaders and congregation.

Now almost every Sunday I made sure I would sit as far back in the overflow

provided by the church because I just wanted to receive the Word and not be

seen. My wife was now a member of two of the church choirs so she mainly sat

with the others. Because she was still a member of the national choir, many

started to lean on her for some musical guidance if needed. Sunday after

Sunday or services throughout the week we attended, I made sure I sat far in the

back. I did help with distribution of items to help families, which was mainly

during holidays, but that was not often. I enjoyed my quiet role in being under

the Word and was happy doing the little I did.

Then one evening after the ending of a night bible study and me sitting way in

the back, the pastor ended his teaching and I could see that he was making his

way towards the back of the church overflow for some reason. I noticed that he

was coming directly towards me. He got to me and he asked me if I would

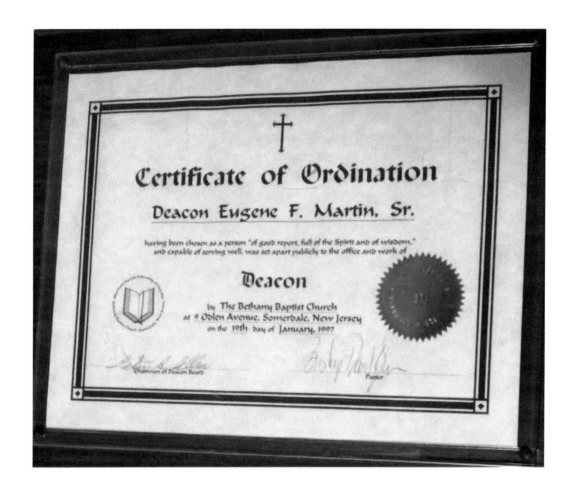

consider becoming one of the Deacons of the church, him starting a new group

under his teachings. I was stunned! Here it was that I tried my best to not be

noticed, while doing everything to not be noticed, but I was still being watched.

He asked me to consider and let him know.

I remember telling my brother Tom and me wondering my I was asked, me

far from what I felt a Deacon was required to be in pleasing a pastor and God

also. Tom looked at me and just answered me by saying, "why not you?" Even

I knew that the pastor surly prayed on my behalf before calling on me and got

his answer from God. Later I let the pastor know I would attend the meeting

planned, as he wanted to answer any questions of concerns myself and others

had. The night of the meeting that included others he had asked, I let him know

that my employment required me to work at night and sometimes on the

weekend. He looked at me and in front of the others, told me that made no difference if I would agree to being taught for the year of teaching and was willing to serve as best I could. I agreed and after walking as a trainee for the year, I was then after a church ceremony along with others, Ordained. I was now an Ordained Deacon which I promised myself that I would not take lightly and do the best I could from the teachings of the pastor and my head Deacon, Peter Allen who taught and guided me.

All do not have the same gifts?

I plainly remember my Bishop many times telling the congregation to " stay in your lane.". Many times throughout the years of my biblical teachings, I was taught that every member had a God given gift to be used. Some having better levels or a certain gift then another, but your gift was necessary in what God had for you to willingly do. I learned to never compare what I could do or could not do watching another. Just keep doing what God had for you to do and to stay in your lane of doing.

Yes it kept my attention how some others could recite scriptures out of the Bible, with ease by memory, while I could not. Others could use big words, showing expressions, when called to pray out loud and I didn't. Some could sing a song with strong feelings compared to others that could cause listeners to shout and bring tears, while other singers couldn't. No matter the level of the person in one's gift, God was happy for you to release what gift you have, and share with to others. My pastors and my older head Deacons helped put those teachings in my head so that I could do the Work planned for me and my gift to use to serve others. I knew to stay in my lane and do not compare.

Making sure to stay the man of my home, family of 512, and
to blood kin when needed.

As I have written in my previous books, I had become the man of the house of
221 at the age of nine years old, trying my best to care for my mom and siblings.
Though I was now a Deacon and my siblings were well up in age as I, and
having spouses and children of their own, I still carried the role of helping one
another when asked. I had been doing so since given the task back in 1957,
and will do it until God, calls me home.

There were times I was asked to preform a duty required by a Deacon to visit
homes, hospitals, nursing homes, and visiting other churches when my Bishop
was to speak, and I did that many times and made the sacrifices needed at
times leaving my blood families, some going through what I call, hard times. For
the many years of me attending my church, I can say to myself, I did the best I
could and gave every task called for me to do, I gave my best.

For the many years of being under the leadership of the Deacon board who
were much older than me, and let me know that I was appreciated, them

knowing my situation and of the others under their care in leading us younger

Deacons, I laid my head down each night knowing God knew I gave my best

during the past hours.

It was sometime hard teachings received from the older board members in

getting one to understand, but they never compared who did what or how much

of one another, for I believe, they knew all had different gifts and levels to be

used. Many times it was said during meetings, our head Deacon would say that

he thought we were the best, and in him saying that, I always took that as my

Bishop looked at us the same way. The best.

Over the years, many of the older senior board leaders and members were

called to glory, moved away, or gave up their leadership because of aging and

health issues. The board leadership was now becoming younger yet

knowledgeable in to the newness of how certain changes were being instilled.

Me being accustomed to the teachings and instructions that got me to the age

and Biblical standing that I was standing now on, allowing me to reach the age

of retirement and doing so during all the test and trials of life that I had to go

through, would question some of the newness being put in place. Many times

when I didn't understand why some of the changes were being made and

because I didn't understand, I stayed in my lane of what I had become

conditioned to do. Being told to " get on board or be left behind ", became a

sentence said to me often, me still staying in my lane. Some of the other

Deacons found the time to do duties in areas outside the church that conflicted

with my family and families of my blood, that wouldn't allow me to sacrifice the

time to attend to what they were doing. I gradually started getting questioned of

my personal life and in my not willing to share with the others, especially much

younger in faith than I, caused me to remained quiet to avoid any arguments or disagreements.. I really felt that if I didn't give an extended answer outside of what I did say to answer the question, the individual would know it was not any of their business and it must definitely be personal.

I was having a heath issue that required me to take medication that made me feel cold all the time. When the decision came to not wear jackets during certain ceremonies, knowing that I had to have on a jacket to stay warm, I didn't want to complain, so I just excused myself of that particular service. Because I was asked to help perform duties of helping with the trustees, who had a separate room during service which was much warmer than the sanctuary, I would help with doing that, but leaving the trustee room to go back into the colder sanctuary if needed. Most of the time because we now had many Deacons, their were enough inside to fulfill the sitting on the bench pew for the Deacons. My letting it be known that it was too cold for my body in the sanctuary seemed to not be a good enough reason to a healthy person.

When I was still working at night and after getting off in the morning, if there was to be a home going service scheduled at the church, they knew I would be in attendance and many times helped speak and read from the pulpit to comfort family and others in attendance. Many times it was only me, a minister, and the person giving the eulogy. I even helped at daytime graveside burials when others were on their jobs of employment, me driving miles to get there. Just me, the undertaker crew, and a minister. Because I enjoyed going to noonday bible study opposed to the evening one, allowing me to care for family and get the sleep needed for night employment, questions were asked about that from others.

Not volunteering to do Saturday morning visiting, when asked, questions were wondered about that. Yes while I was employed and if I, like the others, had a nine to five job, I could have been like many of them in doing things. Yes if I work different hours I would be in view of others to see me doing whatever. Yes if hadn't developed a condition that made me to be on certain medications that made me cold and uncomfortable, yet allowed me to do different from the masses in serving, I would have been seen more. I tried my best by what I could do, while staying in my lane.

The Board Going In A New Direction From My Biblical Training and Teachings.

It was announced that the Deacon board was going in a new direction as to accepting women to become Deacons. I prayed hard about my understanding of who are to become Deacons under my understanding of scripture readings. Because it was a decision made and announced to the congregation with head leadership announcing, my mind was cleared knowing that it was something that didn't agree with, but didn't have to answer to God about the decision. I was ready to just stay in my lane of teaching and continue doing what I was gifted to do.

   Again I thought I was doing the best I could for the times allowed that didn't keep me from taking away from my role as husband, father, and other much needed blood families concerns.

The weight that tried to break my back.   Roman 12:6

   At a monthly Deacon meeting, as we always did, we opened in prayer and sang a song together. All announcements were addressed of the works done by different members during the past month were shared. This was not nothing new that wasn't done, for all the meetings I had attended for years did that. Nothing was different. Now as I earlier mentioned, the board leaders were much younger and some newer as Deacons.

   One of the newer younger Deacons stood to show a graft of what Deacons were doing. The chart showed an A category, B category, and a C category with names of Deacons. The young leader explained that the names in each category represented how much work they were doing in comparison to the others. It was being told to us that those in category B needed to step up to the works that A were doing. It was said that C needed to step up to the works B was doing. What was being said and explained rubbed me the wrong way.

They were now comparing works of one another as to one's gift of calling.

I couldn't believe what I was hearing and seeing. A chart was made of

comparing works. Than I heard and saw my name in the list in the C category. I

waited for the explanation of the charts full meaning then when allowed, voiced

what was on my mind, explaining that I did not like the fact that comparing was

being made. I voiced that I was giving God and the board my best effort and

was upset to what I was seeing. Words were exchanged, a prayer was said, and

an ending song was sang. Immediately at the end of us being excused, I

opened the door and hurt by what I had just witnessed started heading towards

the main church exit. As I was in haste leaving, some members rushed to talk to

me which I could hear them talking, but couldn't listen. After praying hard to

God, in days ahead, I handed in my resignation letter, stepping from the Deacon

Board but not from the church. That last Deacon meeting, after praying hard,

was to be the last time that I had to hear, "get on board or be left behind"

because I didn't fully understand something.   Leaving met that I would not have

to ask another question again to them, causing any confusion.

" THAT DAY"

By Eugene F. Martin, Sr.

Ever since "That Day", I leave the wonder of "That Day" open, I've seen the sun shine brighter, than anytime before. Ever since "That Day".
Ever since "That Day", I've cried many times a good cry, because I made it through those bad cries. Ever since "That Day".
Ever since "That Day", my heart became much lighter, my eyes can see more wider. Ever since "That Day".
As the world falls off my shoulders and drop upon the ground. My steps become more straight, more in rhythm, more in Christ.   Ever since "That Day".

Thank you Jesus

................LOVE............

A greater investment than money, and can draw much more
interest. Show kindness and love to anything, and you'll get a
greater response than can be imagined.

Being an Ordained Deacon means being a Deacon till I die.

I remember clearly some days after becoming an Ordained Deacon, a senior Deacon asked me how I felt now becoming a Deacon. My answer to him was that the only service I now could do that I couldn't before being Ordained, was

now I could serve communion, to others. Even though I have stepped away from the board, the only Deacon duty I gave up was not being with them in the ceremony of the servicing of communion unless they invite me to help.

I can still do everything required and asked of a Deacon, there or attending another churches communion service. Wittiness, visiting, praying, and everything a Deacon is Called to do, that I have not stopped doing.

Thank You For Trusting Me Bishop Evans.

Praying and Serving Others Always, As

Long As My Earthly Body, Has Breath.

PLEASE PRAY FOR ME IF I AM NOT RIGHT, ABOUT AN ORDAINED PERSON, ALWAYS ORDAINED.

THANK YOU PASTORS AND BISHOPS FOR YOUR TEACHINGS.

Humbly Respected Leaders Who Helped Me Along My Path.

Reverend Edgar Wimberly, Father Forrest, Reverend J. H. Hampton, Reverend Ralph Graves Sr., the leader of my wife's Church Bishop William Payne, and the Teacher who made me aware that I had settled in a comfort zone before coming under his/His teaching, Bishop David G. Evans.

These are the Deacons listed below, who set an example of the duties of being a true Deacon in serving others during my "Walking".

Deacon Harold Monroe, Deacon Robert Graves, Sr., Deacon Joseph Witherspoon, Deacon Lewis Keen, Pastor Theodore Smith, Sr., Deacon Peter Allen, Deacon Paul Harris, Deacon Carl Elliott, Deacon Andy Bradley, Deacon John Johnson, Deacon Gabriel Haliburton, and Deacon Wilson Pitts.